BRITAIN'S HERITAGE

Children in the First World War

Mike Brown

AMBERLEY

First published 2017

Amberley Publishing
The Hill, Stroud
Gloucestershire, GL5 4EP

www.amberley-books.com

Copyright © Mike Brown, 2017

The right of Mike Brown to be identified as
the Author of this work has been asserted in
accordance with the Copyrights, Designs and
Patents Act 1988.

ISBN 978 1 4456 6876 5 (paperback)
ISBN 978 1 4456 6877 2 (ebook)

British Library Cataloguing in Publication Data.
A catalogue record for this book is available from
the British Library.

Printed in the UK.

Contents

1
Introduction

When war broke out in August 1914, people thought that it would follow the pattern of past wars; the armed forces would fight the war in some 'foreign field', while civilians, safe at home, would pay for it through taxation. This was soon proved wrong; not only millions of men and women, but even children would be required to 'do their bit' towards the war effort.

They were affected by food shortages, price rises, and rationing. They worked on the land, helping to bring in the harvest, or growing vegetables on allotments at home or in school. Youth organisations such as the Scouts provided patrols to guard the railways, coast watchers, and trumpeters to sound the all-clear, while Guides worked in hospitals, while they, and thousands of others, knitted comforts for the troops.

They would be in the thick of it, with boys serving at the front, having lied about their age, boys and girls working in munitions factories, and everyone under threat from bombardment from the air or the sea.

At the time the lives of ordinary people, and children especially, were not considered important, and histories written after the war reflected this. In this book I hope go some way to putting this right.

Admiral
Sir John Jellicoe.

Hats off to the Flag
we all love and adore,
And give it a mighty
great cheer,
For with gallant Commanders
like this to the fore–
Old England has
nothing to fear.

Admiral Sir John Jellicoe, commander of the Grand Fleet. In the early years of the twentieth century postcards such as this, portraying the leaders of the armed forces, were the equivalent of sports' stars pictures today.

2
Volunteers and Zeppelins

The first effect the war had on most homes was the immediate need to raise a huge army; Lord Kitchener asked for 500,000 volunteers for the British Expeditionary Force (BEF) to go to France. There was a rush to enlist. Up and down the country, thousands of children were suddenly faced with the disappearance of fathers, uncles, and older brothers. As newly formed local units marched out of town, crowds cheered and waved flags as they passed. Many children, especially boys, marched alongside the troops, or followed behind, wishing they were old enough to join up. Many policemen were ex-soldiers who were recalled to the army. To replace them the Government created 'special constables'; men too old to serve who were given a little training, and a striped armband to wear over their ordinary clothes. At first they were seen as figures of fun, and a favourite game for local children was to play tricks on them.

Below left: The classic 1914 recruiting poster by Alfred Leete. Kitchener's eyes and pointing finger seem to be on you, wherever you look at it. Hundreds of thousands flocked to the recruiting offices.
Below right: To fill gaps in the police force caused by the war part-time special constables were recruited. With little training and only an armband, they were the butt of many jokes.

By George - a beastly bomb - what!

"Garn! you said it stood for 'Good Runners'—I don't believe it."

With every available soldier needed in France, people worried about a German invasion. Local men, unable to serve, formed anti-invasion groups, arming themselves to guard their area, much to the delight of the children who would watch their every move. The Government soon took control of these, forming them into the Volunteer Training Corps (VTC). These were men who were too old or too young for the forces, or otherwise unable to serve. At first they wore ordinary clothes with red armbands bearing the letters 'GR' (*Georgius Rex*) to show they were official. Many of them being either elderly, unfit or overweight, the VTC became the butt of many children's jokes; one common example being variations on what GR stood for.

In the first weeks of the war German airships bombed Antwerp. Britain responded by introducing lighting restrictions around all ports and vital targets. By the middle of October 1914, drastic reduction in street lighting in all

Above left: The Volunteer training Corps were a sort of Home Guard. They wore an armband with GR *Georgius Rex*, on it, and much fun was had thinking of alternative meanings of the letters.
Below: Here, the strong cellars of a brewery have been opened as an air raid shelter used by many, including children. Note the lack of any seating or sanitary arrangements; often buckets were provided behind screens.

areas was ordered, to be tightened-up even further one year later. The streets at night became dark, frightening places for many children, and an adventure for others.

In January 1915 death from the skies came to Britain when, on the 19th, two Zeppelins bombed East Anglia, killing four people in Yarmouth and King's Lynn. In mid-April the 'Zepps' returned, bombing Tyneside, the east coast, and East Anglia. On 31 May London was attacked; over a ton of bombs were dropped, mainly on the East End. Such indiscriminate bombing caused injury and death to men, women, and children, and the Zeppelins and their crews became known as the 'baby-killers'. The official advice was that cellars offered the best protection, either in your own home, church crypts, the cellars of shops or local caves such as in Dover, tunnels, or, in London, the Underground stations; here crowds would gather, including a high proportion of children, who would often play games together in the shelters. As the raids continued, more and more people left their refuges to watch the Zepps, the searchlights trying to find them, and the puffs of smoke from our anti-aircraft fire.

A NASTY JAR FOR THE BABY-KILLERS.
German Raider brought down by Gun-fire, somewhere in Essex.
September 24th, 1916.
Sanctioned by Censor, Press Bureau, September 30th, 1916.

The Zeppelin bombings brought civilian deaths, including children, leading to the nickname 'baby-killers'. The postcard shows the spectacle of searchlights, anti-aircraft shells and the airship; many left their shelter to go 'Zepp-watching'.

Did you know?

All German airships were called Zeppelins by the British public, although there were actually three types; the Parseval, the Schutte-Lanze, and the Zeppelin.

Zeppelins were huge; up to 200 metres long. It seemed impossible not to be able to shoot down such a large object, and for a while they seemed to be able to attack at will. Often they flew well above the height that our tiny little fighter aircraft could reach. On moonlit nights when lighting restrictions provided little protection, there would be an exodus of families from the capital to towns such as Brighton.

Then, on the night of 2 September 1916, fighter pilot Lieutenant William Leefe Robinson sighted one of sixteen German airships carrying out a mass raid on England over

Left: A German postcard showing a military Zeppelin of the type that carried out raids over much of Britain. They were truly gigantic; the largest were over 200 metres long, but advances in aircraft technology made them vulnerable.

Below: A photo from 1917 showing a class of girls doing an air drill; this entailed getting under your desk at a given signal, though they don't look very well covered. It all looks very cramped.

Cuffley, Hertfordshire. Robinson attacked at an altitude of 11,500 ft, raking the airship with machine-gun fire. As he was preparing for another attack, the airship burst into flames and crashed at Cuffley. For this action Leefe Robinson was awarded the Victoria Cross; postcard pictures of him were sold, and many children would have collected them.

This action was witnessed by thousands of Londoner Zepp-watchers who, as the airship come down in flames, cheered and sang the national anthem; one even played the bagpipes. Pieces of the crashed balloon were collected up and sold to raise money for the Red Cross; such souvenirs became the prize in many a child's collection. Over the next year the Zeppelins proved ever more vulnerable to our fast-improving defences, and by mid-1917 German aeroplanes had virtually taken over from them, and would carry on the assault until 5 August 1918 – the last German air raid on Britain during the war.

Some schools had special air raid shelters built, such as this one, which has the added protection of sandbags on the top and a steel door.

These aircraft came over during the day, so children at school were under threat. This led to air raid drills in schools; children would be taught to lie on the floor under their desk, or to file down to the school cellars, while some schools in the most threatened areas had special shelters built. These were not needless precautions; on 13 June 1917, during the first daylight raid on London, a bomb fell on Upper North Street primary school in Poplar. The bomb fell through the roof, passing through the girls' class on the top floor and the boys' classroom on the first floor before finally exploding in the infant class on the ground floor, killing eighteen students; sixteen of them aged between four and six.

3
School

Education

There had always been education for those who could afford to pay for it in private schools, but education for all was, in 1914, a comparatively recent thing.

The 1880 Education Act made elementary school compulsory for all children between the ages of five and ten, raised to twelve in 1899. The only fees a council elementary school could charge were for meals; from 1906 another Education Act provided free meals for the least well-off children. A typical lunch might consist of soup, bread and dripping, and sponge pudding. Some schools in the poorer areas also served breakfast: cocoa, porridge, and bread and butter.

Did you know?

In 1914 children could leave school at twelve, and about half of all pupils did so.

A typical urban primary mixed class, wearing a wide variation of clothing, from the poorest through to fairly middle-class clothes. If they stayed on to secondary school, the girls and boys would be taught separately.

Secondary schools were often fee-paying, and in those that were not students still needed money for uniforms, books, etc. Able children might win a scholarship to help pay such fees, but even if this were the case, most poorer families needed the extra wages their children could bring in; yet where possible, many parents realized the boost to later employment of keeping their children at school to fourteen. To cater for this demand, from 1911 new 'central schools' were established in London, Manchester and elsewhere, which provided an improved general education of a practical character – sometimes with an industrial or commercial bias – for pupils between the ages of eleven and fourteen or fifteen. In 1913 the Board of Education came up with the idea of Junior Technical Schools. These were day schools providing two or three-year post-elementary courses for boys and girls aged fifteen or sixteen, combining general

Above right: *The Magnet*, from September 1916, showing Greyfriars – a fictional boys' public school. The two boys are wearing variations of the uniform of such a school; on the left the short jacket and large Eton collar, on the right, a blazer.

Below: A girls' class in a typical classroom with their teacher. Notice the preponderance of white smocks, and the girl on the right in a sailor suit.

education with industrial training. By 1911 surveys showed that about half of all children were staying on at school until they were fourteen, however only 8 per cent stayed until sixteen, and just 2 per cent until they were eighteen.

This is where schooling stood at the outbreak of war, when a great number of children still left school at the end of primary school. By this time the total elementary school population was more than five million.

Wartime conditions made the work of schools difficult; many male teachers volunteered or were called up for military service, to be replaced by women or retired men as the war went on. The needs of the military also affected the children; as fathers and older brothers left for the front, so scholars left school earlier than they would have done to help at home, or to go out to work. Wages rose sharply, attracting many pupils into the workforce; increasing the problems of child labour in factories and farming.

The Classroom

At the front was the teacher's desk, often on a small stage so that the teacher had a better view of the class, or they might sit on a high stool. Next to or behind the teacher's desk was a large wooden blackboard on an easel, on which the teacher would write the lesson with a stick of chalk; textbooks were rarely used.

Classes were bigger with as many as sixty children per class in elementary schools; in smaller schools children of different ages sat together in one or two classrooms. In larger schools, with more pupils, older boys and girls would be taught separately; in many old schools, you can still see the separate entrances for boys and girls marked out.

A very typical desk. On it is a writing slate and slate pencil; the slate marked out for italic writing. In the groove on the desk are two dip pens, used with the inkwell on the left by older pupils.

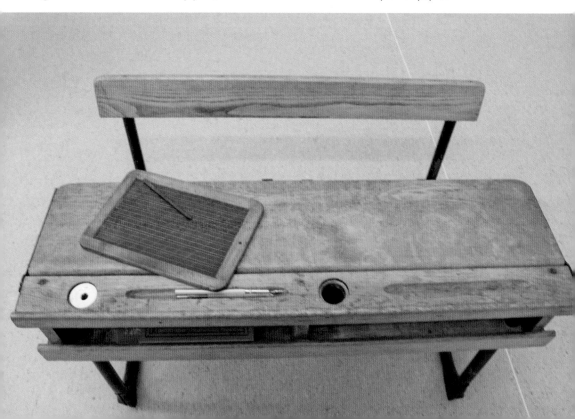

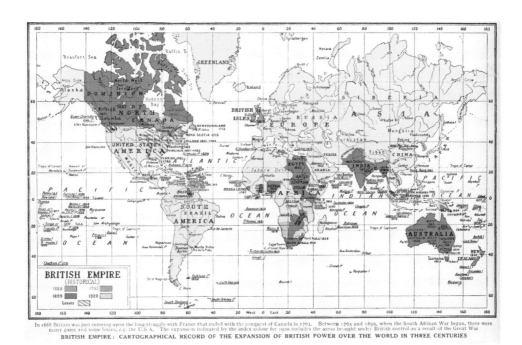

In 1688 Britain was just entering upon the long struggle with France that ended with the conquest of Canada in 1763. Between 1763 and 1899, when the South African War began, there were many gains and some losses, *e.g.* the U.S.A. The expansion indicated by the index colour for 1920 includes the areas brought under British control as a result of the Great War

BRITISH EMPIRE : CARTOGRAPHICAL RECORD OF THE EXPANSION OF BRITISH POWER OVER THE WORLD IN THREE CENTURIES

Every classroom would have a large wall-map of the British Empire. This one from 1920 shows, interestingly, areas of Africa (in orange) gained from Germany after the First World War.

The children's desks were set out in rows, often fixed. The pupils sat on benches, usually with hard wooden seats, sometimes with no back, or with a straight wooden back designed to make you sit up straight. Lack of comfort was also reflected in the lack of central heating; at the front near the teacher would be an iron stove or sometimes a coal fire, which was lit during the winter; those further away from the fire, at the back of the class, could be very cold indeed.

The classroom itself was usually quite plain, often brick walls with a coat of whitewash, no children's work on the walls, and few pictures; just a portrait of the King or the Royal family, a world map, and a religious tract or picture. Younger pupils wrote on a slate using a slate pencil – a piece of slate in the shape of a thin pencil; this left a white mark on the dark slate tablet that could be erased with a little moisture. To rub out any mistakes they had made, it was common for children to spit on the slate. When they had mastered basic writing, the older students used books known as copybooks, in which they wrote with dip pens; basically a wooden stick with a metal nib, which had to be repeatedly dipped into small china inkwells, These sat in a hole cut in the right hand front of the desk, usually next to a groove in which the pen lay when not in use. Being on the right made life difficult for left-handed pupils, but that was not all! Left-handers were usually made to write with their right hand, and would be punished for not doing so with a whack on the offending hand. Keeping the inkwells full was usually the job of the 'ink monitor' – one of the pupils. They would fill the wells from a large bottle of ink, often mixed in the school from powdered ink.

It was hard enough to write neat, joined-up handwriting without leaving blots (drips of ink) or smudging the ink, which took some time to dry, but this was made even harder by the crude pens and poor quality ink.

Above: Another girls' class. This one has, for the time, a lot of pictures on the wall; notice the slates, this time slotted into a special recess at the front of the desks.

Below left: The national anthems of the allies; most of the flags are recognisable. The black eagle on the yellow flag is the old Russian Imperial eagle. These tunes would be played in schools on special occasions.

Subjects

Whilst many of the subjects taught would be familiar to today's pupils, the method of teaching was very different. Much time was spent learning facts off by heart; the teachers wrote lists of them on the blackboard, which the children copied and memorized. They would then chant them out loud, either as a class or individually, from memory; and woe betide anyone who got them wrong. Punishments included being kept in and writing lines, but there was also physical punishment; a rap on the knuckles with a ruler, or over the hand or bottom with the cane, or a leather strap, or simply a smack on the legs or bottom.

A report for one girl attending one of the new central schools lists her various subjects. These included, under English; reading, writing, spelling, composition, grammar, literature and recitation.

Recitation meant learning poetry off by heart and then reciting it to the class. A good example is this excerpt from 'Big Steamers' by Rudyard Kipling. This was a great favourite at the time, and would have been learned by thousands of children;

"Oh, where are you going to, all you Big Steamers,
With England's own coal, up and down the salt seas?"
"We are going to fetch you your bread and your butter,
Your beef, pork, and mutton, eggs, apples, and cheese."
　"And where will you fetch it from, all you Big Steamers,
And where shall I write you when you are away?"
"We fetch it from Melbourne, Quebec, and Vancouver.
Address us at Hobart, Hong-Kong, and Bombay."
　"But if anything happened to all you Big Steamers,
And suppose you were wrecked up and down the salt sea?"
"Why, you'd have no coffee or bacon for breakfast,
And you'd have no muffins or toast for your tea."
　"Then what can I do for you, all you Big Steamers,
Oh, what can I do for your comfort and good?"
"Send out your big warships to watch your big waters,
That no one may stop us from bringing you food."
　For the bread that you eat and the biscuits you nibble,
The sweets that you suck and the joints that you carve,
They are brought to you daily by All Us Big Steamers
And if any one hinders our coming you'll starve!"

Mathematics included arithmetic, algebra, and geometry; then there was history, geography, French, science, art, and commercial subjects; shorthand, book-keeping, typewriting, commercial training, needlework, handicraft and domestic subjects. The latter included knitting, cooking and other skills such as ironing, looking after babies and the sick. Only girls learned domestic subjects. Practical lessons for boys included technical drawing, carpentry, bricklaying and metalwork. These commercial lessons usually took place in the afternoon. At some schools, especially in country districts, both boys and girls were taught gardening.

PE (physical exercise) was usually done in the playground or the hall with the children standing in rows in their ordinary clothes, doing things like knee bends, etc. Playing organized games such as hockey, football or cricket became a problem during the war, as playing fields were lost.

Food shortages across the country meant everyone, including schools, had to cut back. In many schools the boys broke up a large piece of the playground and used it for growing vegetables; in one school, for instance, in 1918, over a ton of potatoes were raised, as well as large quantities of other vegetables. In another the elder girls dug up and cultivated a large piece of their playground, and each produced, in addition to other vegetables, about ½ cwt. of potatoes, paying for their own seeds.

In 1917, the Government introduced the Food Economy campaign to encourage the nation to save food. Ministry officials visited schools where they addressed pupils between nine and fourteen years old, telling them that the demands for economy were directed at them

Above: Boys doing PE in the playground of a very typical school using barbells. There is no games kit, they have merely taken off their jackets.

Left: Public schoolboys playing football. Knee-length shorts were worn by most boys up to the age of twelve, and by older boys for sports. Notice the boy on the right, in blazer and cap.

Eton schoolboys growing food. In many schools part of the playing fields or playground would be dug over and planted with vegetables; often the older children would have gardening lessons.

as much as older people. The main idea was not just to encourage children to eat less, but to teach them that eating slowly was the best way to preserve their health and conserve food. Help was also rendered by elementary school teachers, impressing upon their elder pupils the need for avoiding waste, whilst at the same time indicating practical methods of making the most of food.

Did you know?

In 1918 the elder boys in rural districts were allowed six weeks extra summer holiday to assist in gathering in the harvest.

The older scholars also did their share towards food production by working in the fields during the busiest times, before school and in the evening. During 1917 the Government asked children to collect horse chestnuts for munition making and blackberries for jam for soldiers (for which they were paid 3*d* per pound). In the towns and cities waste paper was collected. In some boarding schools personal sacrifice was called for; all sugar in tea was given up and cakes and/or jam disappeared. In many areas prizes were given up and a badge or certificate was awarded instead.

Many types of war work were done in schools; the girls knitted 'comforts' – scarves, socks, balaclava helmets, etc. – to send to the troops, while some near military camps undertook the mending of uniforms. Others collected jam, chocolate, books, and other comforts. Help was also given to the Red Cross in the form of gifts to local hospitals.

Each year on Empire Day (24 May) and at Christmas, scholars would collect for tobacco and comforts for soldiers and sailors, or footballs, books or dart boards, while Christmas parcels were sent out to the school's 'old boys' serving in the forces.

Left: As the war continued, sacrifices were demanded from the public to help towards its vast cost. In many places, such as the LCC, school prizes were given up to be replaced by certificates such as this.
Below: A certificate from the Overseas Club, 1916, given to children who had sent Christmas presents to members of the armed forces. Notice the Scouts and Guides at the top.

A second focus of relief work was the Belgian refugees who had come to Britain. In some cases a school would undertake to support a family living locally, getting a house free or at a reduced rent, supplying their clothes, and raising money for their food. On a smaller scale children might collect for good causes such as the Fund for Relief of Belgian children, the Royal National Lifeboat Institution, Queen Mary's Needlework Guild, Church Army Huts, the YMCA, or the St Dunstan's Hostel for Blinded Sailors and Soldiers.

Many schools joined the War Savings Association, which raised money to pay for the war in the form of National Savings Certificates. These cost 15 shillings and 6 pence each (around £50 today), but you did not have to buy them all in one go. You started with a card on to which you could stick 6*d* 'savings stamps'. When the total reached 15/6d the card was exchanged for a certificate, which could, after five years, be cashed in for £1. Teachers, on a set day of the week, would take cash from the pupils in exchange for savings stamps.

Right: A National savings stamp. These were often sold in schools to be stuck into the card, shown in the next illustration.
Below left: A War savings card. This was filled up with thirty-one sixpenny savings stamps, often purchased in schools. When filled it was exchanged for a savings certificate, worth twenty shillings after the war.
Below right: One way girls could help with the war effort was by knitting comforts for the troops, such as scarfs, balaclava helmets and socks. Knickers then meant shorts.

NAUGHTY NETTA'S KNITTING KNICKERS
FOR THE SEAT OF WAR.

4
Helping with the War Effort

NATIONAL

REGISTRATION

ACT, 1915.

In 1915, with conscription in mind, the people were recorded in what was called National Registration, and cards like this were issued to all adults.

The most direct way that boys became involved with the war was to join the forces. Before conscription was introduced in 1916, Britain relied on volunteers to make up the hundreds of thousands of troops needed at the front. The minimum age to join the army was eighteen, but many lads lied about their age to fight for their country, and many recruiting sergeants turned a blind eye to volunteers who were clearly underage. At the time most people didn't have birth certificates, so it was easy to lie about your age. It was less easy to lie about your size, but as the minimum height for recruits was only 5 feet 3 inches, many youngsters had no trouble making the grade. One *Punch* cartoon from 1915 ran, 'Officer (to boy of thirteen who, in his effort to get taken on as a bugler, has given his age as sixteen): "Do you know where boys go who tell lies?" Applicant: "To the front, sir."'

The youngest known British soldier in the First World War was twelve-year-old Sidney Lewis, who fought at the Battle of the Somme in 1916. The youngest to die was Private John Condon, aged fourteen, killed in the Second Battle of Ypres, in May 1915, when the Germans used poison gas for the first time.

To facilitate conscription, National Registration was introduced in 1916. Adults were issued with an identity card; in this way the flood of underage soldiers was stopped. At the same time a movement began to bring back the boys already in the forces, and the War Office agreed that parents could obtain their return if they could prove their sons were underage.

The most famous young British serviceman was John Travers Cornwell, commonly known as Jack or Boy Cornwell. In October 1915, without telling his parents, fifteen-year-old Cornwell joined the Royal Navy where he trained as a Gun Layer; part of a gun crew. He was promoted to 'Boy Seaman First Class', aboard HMS *Chester*.

On 31 May 1916, at the Battle of Jutland, *Chester* came under intense fire from four German cruisers, and Cornwell's gun received at least four near hits. The rest of Cornwell's gun crew were killed or mortally wounded; although himself badly wounded with steel splinters in

Above: An illustration from a wartime children's book, showing sixteen-year-old John Cornwell, standing mortally wounded at his gun at the battle of Jutland. He was posthumously awarded the Victoria Cross.

Right: A photograph which reputedly shows John 'Boy' Cornwell. Most historians now believe it to be one of his brothers. He became such a role model for boys that the Boy Scouts instituted the Cornwell Scout badge for courage.

his chest, he stayed at his post until *Chester*, having received eighteen hits, and with only one of its large guns still operative, pulled out of the fight. Cornwell was found still at his gun, waiting for orders. He was taken to Grimsby General Hospital, where he died on 2 June before his mother arrived. He was awarded Britain's highest award, the Victoria Cross.

When war broke out in 1914, a new force called the Volunteer Training Corps or VTC was set up to defend the homeland. Although not planned for, many local VTC units accepted boys too young to join up, and in July 1915, the VTC command issued a retrospective order allowing the formation of Cadet Companies consisting of youths between the ages of fourteen and seventeen, who were only to mix with the adult VTC for drill and training purposes. They were allowed to wear a uniform, which had badges on the shoulders marked 'V.T.C. CADETS'. When they reached seventeen, they moved up to the adult VTC.

Another way of working for the war effort was in a munitions factory; by 1915 there were 8,000 boys employed at Woolwich Arsenal. It was estimated that 35 per cent of working boys were engaged in war work, and that a similar proportion of girls were either doing war work or work that before the war had been done by boys. The increase in the wages of small boys was

Below left: A Sea Scout and his father. Sea Scouts did much war-related work, including coast watching (for which a badge was awarded). Older ones also helped crew patrol boats.
Below right: An advert from a boys' comic from 1918 encouraging boys to join the Volunteer Regiment Cadets, which had been the Volunteer Training Corps Cadets until its name changed in 1915.

ALONZO TODD

will arrive like this when he is called up, because he

IS
NOT

A CADET.

If you are not a Cadet, apply at once to "C.A.V.R., Judges' Quadrangle, Law Courts, W.C. 2," who will send you particulars of your nearest Corps.

enormous; standard wages went up by 40 or 50 per cent. Many boys who left school after the war broke out were able to get jobs at once at anything from £1 or 25s a week. In munitions factories boys were earning 30s a week and upwards soon after leaving school. One boy of sixteen was quoted as earning £3 19s a week at piece rates, and this, it was stated, was not an isolated case.

This, however, came at a cost; at Woolwich Arsenal for instance, boys worked from either 8 a.m. to 8 p.m., or from 8 p.m. to 8 a.m. – a twelve-hour day, and on alternate weeks a twelve-hour night. Many of them lived at a distance, and, owing to the bad train service, had to get up at 5.30 or 6 a.m. and could not get to bed before 10 or 10.30 p.m., giving just seven hours in bed for a boy of fourteen! The average small boy was, in many cases, earning as much as or even more than his father did before the war, with some becoming the family breadwinner. However, in the majority of cases, much of the money was simply wasted on unnecessary things. Social workers were worried by this; many of the boys had, since leaving school, been repeating one action – that of testing cartridges. When the war is over, they argued, the boys would be dismissed, and what would they have learnt that would be of use to them? One answer to the problem was continuing education in the form of evening classes, but only about 10 per cent of boys attended an evening school before the war. Once the war began, owing to overtime, this dropped to 8 per cent. Many social workers argued that all children between fourteen and eighteen should be compelled to attend classes after leaving day-school.

NATIONAL SERVICE ACT VOLUNTEERS BETWEEN THE AGES OF 16 & 61 WANTED FOR THE FOLLOWING TRADES

" Yes, an' by the time I'm sixteen, the blinking war'll be over ! "

The early rush to join up created a shortage of workers in munitions factories and other vital war work. The Government launched a campaign to recruit workers to these key jobs.

Other children did war-related activities through youth groups such as the Boys' Brigade, the Boy's Life Brigade, the Jewish Lads' Brigade, and the Boy Scouts. The Scouts are an excellent example of the popularity of youth movements at the time. In September 1909, less than two years after being formed, the first national Boy Scout meeting was held at Crystal Palace in London, which over 10,000 Scouts attended. This included girls calling themselves Girl Scouts. The following year the Girl Guides were formed, followed in 1916 by the Wolf Cubs.

As a quasi-military body the Scouts were most frequently used by the authorities. They began their war work immediately; during August 1914, patrols of Scouts assisted the military by patrolling the coast, checking permits in restricted areas, and keeping watch for invasion. Inland, others guarded railway stations and bridges, under the supervision of a military officer. Others guarded telephone and telegraph lines, reservoirs and other locations of importance, or worked as despatch riders and signallers. Some helped at soldiers' canteens and recreation rooms, while others did orderly and fatigue work at war hospitals, and many assisted with the harvest and the fishing industry.

Above left: With the departure of the army for France in 1914, Britain's coast was left poorly defended from invasion, and the Boy Scouts stepped in to guard railway bridges and other key points, including the coast itself.

Above right: A typical group of munitions workers (note the shell cases at the front); several of the 'women' are young girls, and there are two very young boys amongst them.

Did you know?

From late 1917 many Scouts took on air raid duties, including aircraft spotting and reporting, escorting people to air raid shelters and fire fighting, while Scout buglers sounded the 'All Clear' after air raids.

Throughout the war the Scouts collected waste paper for the Prince of Wales' National Relief Fund. They collected money for Scout motor-ambulances for France, and gathered wild seasonal crops such as rosehips and sphagnum moss for medicines, and chestnuts for munitions.

Girl Guides also took on many roles. They made, collected and packaged up clothing for men at the front, prepared hostels and first-aid dressing stations for the victims of air raids or accidents, kept allotments, and helped in hospitals, munitions factories and government offices.

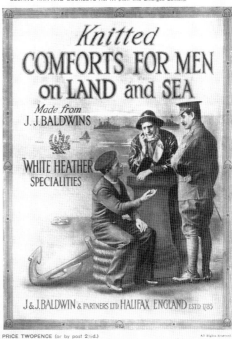

BEEHIVE KNITTING BOOKLETS No. 17. (New and Enlarged Edition).

Knitted
COMFORTS FOR MEN
on LAND and SEA

Made from
J. J. BALDWINS

WHITE HEATHER
SPECIALITIES

J & J. BALDWIN & PARTNERS LTD HALIFAX ENGLAND ESTD. 1785

PRICE TWOPENCE (or by post 2½d.)

Above left: A family photo; the daughter (on the left) is in the Women's Auxiliary Army Corps, Dad is a merchant seaman. The son is a Scout, proudly holding his bugle, which he would have used to sound the 'All Clear'.

Above right: Baldwin's pattern booklet for knitted comforts for the services. Girls were encouraged to knit, amongst other things, mittens, gloves, caps, socks, sea boot stockings, waistcoats, and body belts.

Right: A group of nurses and helpers in a war hospital. Note the three Girl Guides; this was one of the many ways that guides and others helped with the war effort.

5
Playtime

Games

The lack of cars made the streets far safer than they are today. In the towns the streets were the playgrounds, and many games were played there. Often all the local children joined in so that games might have twenty or more participants. Popular street games included hide and seek, 'It' (and variations such as British Bulldog, off-ground touch, and sticky toffee), skipping, hopscotch, football, cricket, running races, etc.; most of which required no more special equipment than a ball, or in the case of cricket, a crudely-shaped piece of board. Skipping needed a rope – often an old piece of clothes line – and hopscotch a grid drawn out on the pavement – sometimes in chalk, sometimes with a

Below left: A nurse's outfit, either purchased or homemade, would be a must-have addition to any little girls dressing up box.
Below right: Father is proudly wearing his Volunteer Training Corps uniform (note the GR armband), while the little boy is wearing (equally proudly) his own version of the same uniform.

EYES RIGHT!

Most children would create their uniforms and weapons for playing 'war' out of whatever came to hand, such as this rather motley crew.

piece of old, soft brick. Knock Down Ginger, on the other hand, required nothing more than the cheek to knock on someone's door, and the speed to run away before you were caught.

'War' had always been a popular game, especially amongst the boys. Now with the advent of real war, it became even more so. Better-off children had small uniforms and pop-guns, poorer children made caps and puttees from newspapers, swords and guns from sticks and the military band made up of old biscuit-tin drums and penny whistles. The problem was that nobody wanted to play the Germans; the younger kids and/or the girls might be forced to take on the role, but this rather diminished the glory of beating them.

Toys

The most popular toys at the turn of the century were pull-along trains and boats, clock-work toys (again trains were popular) and toy soldiers; some in wood, which were large, others, smaller, were in lead or tinplate. Many dolls' faces were made of china or pottery, their bodies often made of stuffed cloth, as were soft toys.

There were very few motor cars in existence, and the amount of toy cars reflected this. Yachts that could be sailed on the local boating lake were popular, coming in a great range of sizes, as did kites. Spinning tops, skipping ropes, hoops, footballs and marbles were

Above left: The sailor suit from a studio portrait. The child's sailor suit was all the rage both before and during the war for both boys and girls. Pull-along toys such as this farm cart were very popular for younger children.
Above right: A grand selection of boxed soldiers and canons forming a battlefield commanded by both boys and girls, from November 1916.

particular favourites. Card games and board games were popular; old maid, happy families and snap, amongst the first, and snakes and ladders, and ludo the second; blow-football was one of the more popular new games. There were no battery powered or electronic toys, and plastic was a rarity.

Before the war, Germany had been the world's most important producer of children's toys, which they exported to Europe and the USA; many toys bought in Britain were German imports. With the war German goods were shunned, including old favourites like Steiff bears. This gave British and French manufacturers a chance to build up their markets; toys and other products were proudly labelled 'British Made'.

War-related toys were soon in the shops; many saw them as a way to strengthen children's involvement with the war effort. Production of war toys reached numbers never-before seen. Toy soldiers had long been popular, but often in red coats; now they were in khaki, and there were pull-along dreadnought battleships, field guns and howitzers, Maxim machine guns, armoured motor cars, horse-drawn Red Cross wagons and even complete

Did you know?

War-related toys proved most popular in 1914, but by 1917 they were losing favour as war-weariness and disillusionment spread throughout the civilian population.

I'se not afraid of the Germans.
Ze n'ai pas peur des Boches!

A paper hat and a crude wooden sword were all that was needed for most children to be able to play war. Any model German soldiers were likely to fare little better than these in such games.

field hospitals. Later child-size Army, Royal Flying Corps and Navy uniforms were available, and, when the army took to wearing helmets, small children's versions were soon in the toy shops. For girls, Red Cross nurses' uniforms were most popular, as were dolls in nurses' uniforms, or teddy bears in patriotic uniforms. My wife's grandfather remembered a 'Little Willie' toy he had; the name was a popular form of lampooning the German Emperor Wilhelm. You pulled a string at the bottom and his arms and legs shot up as if he had been blown up.

As the war ground on, many factories stopped making toys; the growing demands of the weapons industry meant raw materials became harder to get for civilian use. Toys were increasingly hand made, either by parents or family, or by injured soldiers and sailors; the Lord Roberts Memorial Workshops were set up to teach them toy-making skills as a form of rehabilitation and a way of earning money.

Comics

The first comics, sometimes known as 'penny dreadfuls', began to appear in the late nineteenth century. One such was *Ally Sloper's Half Holiday*, which first appeared in 1884 but was still going strong at the start of the First World War, only ceasing publication in 1916. Like all the early comics, *Ally Sloper's Half Holiday* was actually aimed at an adult readership, although they might have a children's section, as most adult magazines did. The first comics

Below left: *The Magnet* – a boys' comic, this one from 1916. It was full of stories about the pupils of Greyfriars public school, including its most famous scholar, Billy Bunter.
Below right: By 1917, the *Girl's Own Paper* had amalgamated with *Woman's Magazine*. The resulting magazine was aimed very much at teenage girls, with articles on fashion, needlework, cooking, etc.

THE RAINBOW. 1D. THE CHILDREN'S PAPER THAT PARENTS APPROVE OF.

No. 168. Vol. 4.   PRICE ONE PENNY.   April 28, 1917.

The Rainbow comic from 1917. Aimed at very young children, the war was hardly mentioned, as parents tried to insulate them from the conflict.

specifically for younger children didn't start being published until *Rainbow* in 1914; these proved most successful and soon most comics were aimed at this younger age group.

Comics for older children at the time of the war tended to be more like magazines, with long illustrated stories. These included *The Boy's Own Paper*, first published in 1879, by the Religious Tract Society. As might be expected, it contained stories about plucky youths battling honourably against underhand, oafish opponents (often foreigners), in sporting, historical, and public school settings. By the First World War the paper was aimed at better-off boys, and had articles and stories by the likes of Captain Webb, (first man to swim the English Channel), the cricketer W. G. Grace, Robert Baden-Powell, (founder of the Boy Scouts), and great authors such as Jules Verne and Arthur Conan Doyle. As well as such sporting and literary contributions, there were articles on keeping animals and pets, on historical, geographical and scientific subjects, and on a whole range of subjects of interest to a teenage boy, such as stamp collecting, although girls were rarely mentioned.

Similar magazines were *The Captain* and *The Magnet*; this had tales of Greyfriars Public School and its inhabitants – Bob Cherry, Harry Wharton, and of course Billy Bunter.

Girls had, amongst other comics and magazines, *The Girl's Own Paper*; also published by the Religious Tract Society it first appeared in 1880. By 1917, it had joined forces with *Woman's Magazine*, becoming *The Girl's Own Paper and Woman's Magazine*. During the war it carried short stories, a problems page, and articles on fashion, cookery, housecraft – 'the art of ironing', gardening – 'the garden in July', and even articles on keeping poultry, etc.

Above left: The war played a very large part in the books and comics of older children, this early volume relating tales of heroism and British pluck was typical of many.

Above right: *Dreadnoughts of the Dogger; stories of the war at sea*, including 'the Menace of the Mines', 'Brave as a Briton' and 'What Mark found in the Pigeon Loft'!

More recognisable as comics were titles such as *Chips* featuring Weary Willie, *Lot-o-Fun*, *Comic Life*, *The Funny Wonder*, *Picture Fun* and of course, *The Rainbow*. These often featured stories of their characters outwitting oafish, greedy, and unsportsmanlike behaviour by Germans.

Books

Like war-related toys, children's books and comics were seen as a means of strengthening their identification with the war effort. This had long been a popular form of children's literature, with many books about heroic and steadfast children of the past, either real or fictional.

Popular children's writers included Frances Hodgson Burnett, who wrote *A Little Princess*, *Little Lord Fauntleroy* and *The Secret Garden*, although the latter was not the success it is today. Sir Henry Rider Haggard (better known as H. Rider Haggard) wrote tales of derring-do including *King Solomon's Mines*, and *She* in the late Victorian times, which were still popular in the war and long after. *Scouting for Boys* had been written in 1908 by Robert Baden Powell and soon became a best seller, second only to the Bible.

6
Clothing

The vast differences in wealth amongst the population were very much reflected in the clothes children wore. Few working-class children would ever have new clothes; children's clothes especially were hand-me-downs, passed from one brother, sister, or cousin to a smaller or younger relative as they grew out of them. As such, clothing was often a poor fit; too big when you first got it, too small when you passed it on. Some items of clothing could be hand-sewn or knitted, and repairs, patches and alterations were the norm. When clothes for these children had to be bought, it was almost always from one of the second-hand clothing shops, which abounded in the poorer districts. Very few working-class children would have more than one suit of clothes; underwear, shirts, pinafores, etc., were commonly rinsed and hung out each night, ready to be worn again next day.

Below left: In their Sunday best outfits. The boy on the left – it *is* a boy – is typically wearing a dress and strapped shoes. Both young boys and girls wore dresses until the age of two or three.
Below right: A linen suit for a boy from four to six years old, from August 1917. Short trousers, or knickers as they were called, were worn by all boys up to the age of twelve.

Thus fashion was something that only the better-off children could aspire to. At the time clothes fell into two categories – children's clothes and adult clothes – and apart from size there was often little difference between them. The teenager did not yet exist as a separate entity; you went straight from childhood to adulthood at twelve. Boys would wear short trousers until they reached that age; getting your first long trousers was a rite of passage. The rest of a boy's outfit would, in many ways, be a cut-down version of the man's version; even the boys' school cap was worn in a larger size by men. Similarly with the girls; their skirts were knee-length until about the age of twelve or thirteen, then the hemline would drop, reaching ankle-length by about fifteen or sixteen when they would wear versions of their mother's clothes. Up to this point it was very common to wear a white cotton pinafore over the dress; this was often like a smock, worn to protect the dress and keep it clean.

Only the youngest or better-off children wore shoes. Almost everyone else wore ankle boots, especially for outdoors; many side roads were unmade, and the prevalence of horse traffic created its own dangers for the poorly-shod. Once again, many poorer families could not afford more than one pair of boots for each child, and it was not uncommon for children to miss school because their one pair of boots were at the menders, or to see children playing barefoot in the street in good weather to save shoe-leather.

One great difference between girls' and women's clothing was their underwear. The Victorian fashion had been for women to have the 'hour-glass' figure – large around the hips and chest, with a tiny waist. This had been accomplished with the use of tightly laced corsets, which so constricted the waist that eating and even breathing were difficult – which explains why women were always 'swooning' in Victorian stories. Calls to prevent this led to the formation of the 'Dress Reform Movement', which aimed to free women, and especially young girls, from such corsetry and the accompanying layers of unhealthy underclothes. From this emerged the gym slip; a waist-less tunic, which, as the name suggests, allowed girls the physical freedom

By the age of sixteen or so, both boys and girls were wearing clothes very much like their parents'. According to the back of the photo, the boy is eighteen years old and his sister sixteen.

Mother and daughter, 1918, showing the great difference between women's and girls' clothing. Notice the different hemlines and mum's tight waist, as opposed to the daughter's waist-less dress.

to do sports, and became widespread in schools in the inter-war years. It also led to the liberty bodice; an undergarment for women and especially girls invented in the late nineteenth century as an alternative to the corset. This was a simply shaped sleeveless top, made of warm, fleecy fabric, with no bones, unlike corsets, giving far greater freedom of movement, from where it derived its name. They usually had buttons to fasten on to the wearer's underpants, generally called drawers – these were like long shorts, elasticated around the waist and legs.

Boys, after romper suits, would move on to shorts; long shorts, reaching almost to the knee – confusingly called knickers (short for knickerbockers) – that were often part of a suit, sometimes tucked into long socks. The jacket might be a Norfolk jacket, single-breasted, with box pleats back and front, with a belt, or an Eton jacket, (named after the public school), single-breasted and short. Underneath would be a shirt with a large Eton collar worn outside the jacket, and a tie; usually a school tie, with large 1-inch horizontal stripes. Sometimes younger boys would have a lace-edged collar.

Did you know?

Babies and small children, both boys and girls, wore dresses up to the age of two, three or even older; after this girls continued with dresses, or overall dresses, while boys went into one or two piece romper suits.

A very popular alternative for both boys and girls was the sailor suit, especially in the summer. These took several forms, the main thing being the collar which flared to a 'flap' at the back, like the traditional sailor's collar designed to protect their uniform from their tarred pigtail. Very often the collar would be in blue with white piping, or vice versa, just like the real thing. In the winter, there were even reefer-style short overcoats.

Standard Clothing

Providing uniforms for the services – by now numbering in the millions – brought cloth shortages for civilian use throughout the spring and summer of 1917. To curb the inevitable price rises that followed, the Government decided to produce 'standard cloth'; a cheap material for use in clothing for poorer people. At first it was thought that one type of cloth should be made available at a fixed price. In the event, only the broad details governing the manufacture of the cloth were to be laid down, so that it would be possible to introduce a reasonably large variety of patterns so as to avoid an undesirable uniformity. It was believed that this cloth could be produced at about 6 shillings a yard, and using it clothiers could make suits and sell them at a fixed price to the retailer, who would in turn supply them at a fixed price, for all sizes of garment, to the public. It was hoped to produce suits for boys, costing approximately 22s 6d for younger boys, 30s for older boys, and 40s for youths.

Below left: The liberty bodice offered a freedom of movement that allowed girls to take part in physical exercise and sports. The buttons round the waist allowed the bodice to be attached to other underwear.
Below right: A charming little girl in a studio photograph. Note the sailor cap and reefer jacket, the bucket and wooden spade – vital equipment for the seaside – and especially the long boots. By 1918 leather shortages would restrict the length of boots.

Spring styles for girls between ten and fourteen years old, from April 1917; note the just-below knee-length skirts. These are dress-makers' patterns, rather than from a shop catalogue; most children's clothes were hand-made.

At the beginning of January 1918, it was reported that the supply of 200,000 yards of standard cloth for youths' and boys' suits at 5s 3d per yard had been arranged. There were to be four grades of cloth; the best quality was a twill serge in blue, black and brown, for youths' ready-to-wear suits. Grade two cloth was used for youths' and boys' overcoats. Grade three cloth consisted of twenty-four cheviot tweeds and eight mixture tweeds, grey, brown, blue and black for youths' suits and boys' Rugby suits. Rugby suits, named after the school, consisted of a jacket that buttoned up almost to the neck, a waistcoat, and knee-length shorts. Finally, Grade four was made up of eighteen tweeds in grey and brown for boys' knickerbocker suits; these were suits with long loose shorts, which usually did up around the knee.

At the beginning of September 1918, a delay in the appearance of standard suits and other standard articles of wear was reported, due to unexpected and exceptionally heavy military demands on production. However, 'a certain quantity of standard hosiery for women, girls, and boys should be on sale by the end by the end of this month, and a limited amount of underwear for women and children early in October'.

In spite of all the promises, very little standard clothing was available until after the war; in the meantime, patches and repairs in children's clothes became normal, and not only for the less well-off. When it did at last appear, it was expensive; in June 1919 *The Times* reported complaints about the excessive prices asked for even the lowest quality clothing. 'For a suit for a small boy £3 is asked, a sum which represents a week's wage to many artisans.' Standard cloth soon gained a bad reputation; after just a few washes or cleanings, it became covered in little balls of fluff, and the dye was notoriously poor; often turning a dull purple, whatever colour it had started out.

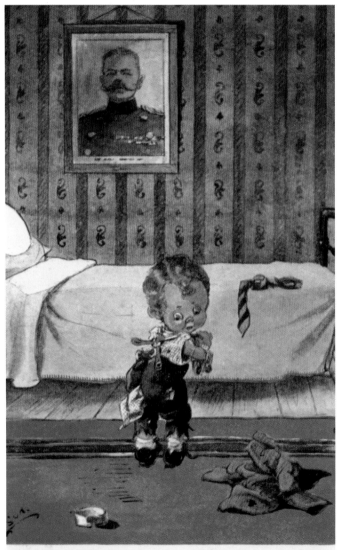

Anyhow, they've got to last till the War's over.

By 1917, cloth shortages meant that mended and patched clothes, once the preserve of the poor, were becoming increasingly seen amongst the middle classes.

Summer frocks for girls aged twelve to eighteen years old, from June 1915. By this age the hem is around mid-calf length, dropping to ankle length at the age of eighteen.

Footwear

By 1917 British manufacturers not only supplied boots to the British army, but to the Russian forces, and later the American army as well. This meant, as usual, that the civilian population was sent to the back of the queue as far as footwear was concerned. Consequently they endured hardships, which became a source not only of discontent but of positive danger to the health, both of the children and of the adult population. Shoes and boots were repaired, then the repairs repaired. The Board of Trade under the 'Leather Controller', Frederick Marquis, devised a range of civilian war-time boots and shoes for all ages, for men, women, and children, and had these boots made to a high standard of durability and reliability and at a fixed price. The profit margins of the wholesalers and retailers were also fixed, thus keeping the cost down.

Young siblings, the youngest in a sailor suit with knickers (shorts), the girl in a dress, typically with a white lace-edged collar, and the oldest in another sailor suit. All three are in ankle boots and over-ankle socks.

7
Food

There was a vast difference between the diets of the rich and the poor. The rich would eat a dinner of several courses; the poor commonly had only enough food for one decent meal a day. Poor children were consequently undernourished, and markedly smaller than their better-off equivalents, and many suffered from problems such as rickets.

There were no freezers or refrigerators in homes; most food was bought on a daily basis. Food was far more seasonal and it was also much more local. Food from other countries was rare; curry was very popular, as was rice, but pizza or hamburgers were virtually unheard of. Vegetables were often boiled to mush, and boiled meat was common; 'Boiled beef and carrots' was a popular song of the time.

Compared with today's fare, food was far stodgier, with lots of steamed puddings – both savoury and sweet – such as steak and kidney pudding, and spotted dick. There were some prepared foods; tinned soup, and a few tinned vegetables, corned beef and sardines, etc., but on the whole meals were prepared from scratch each day, or from yesterday's leftovers.

The following is a typical day's meals for a well-to-do, middle class household of the period, which would have been eaten by both the adults and the children, (with the exception of the coffee). Breakfast consisted of fried bacon, sardines, bread, butter, marmalade, tea or

A fine piece of period propaganda; even with the shortages, the British could eat nourishing food – beef, potatoes and oatmeal – while the Germans were eating sausages whose contents were a mystery (best left unsolved).

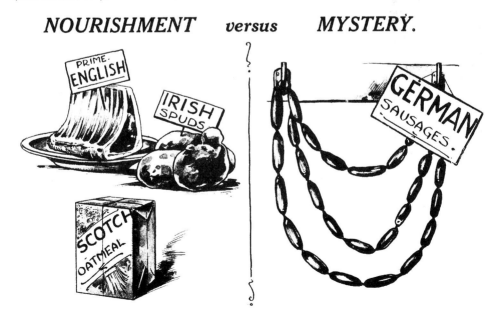

NOURISHMENT *versus* MYSTERY.

coffee. For dinner; roast mutton, jelly, potatoes, cabbage, gooseberry tart and pancakes. Tea would be bread and butter, cakes, jam, marmalade and tea, while supper consisted of cheese, biscuits, bread, butter, cakes, cocoa or milk. On the other hand, a typical day's meals for a manual worker's family comprised of, for breakfast; bread, bacon, butter and tea. Dinner would be bacon and eggs, potatoes, bread (no butter) and tea. Tea would be bread and butter, and tea and, for supper, another cup of tea. Notice the reliance on bread, bacon and tea.

There were two main forms of takeaway; fish and chips, and pie and mash; the latter shops sold meat pies with mashed potatoes and a green 'liquor' gravy. They also sold jellied eels. Takeaways were very much working-class fare; often both mum and dad would be working, and the oldest child would look after the 'littl'uns', often sharing a 'penn'orth' of chips between them, or a piece of bread each. For the better off there were, of course, many teashops and 'refreshment rooms', cafes, and restaurants.

No Cakes, no Jam, no Sugar, no nuffin ! "

Sugar and wheat shortages robbed the table of many of what children would regard as the finer things in life, as portrayed here by Donald McGill.

We did not, and still do not, grow enough food in this country to feed us; about one-third of it has to be imported from other countries. Some food is not commonly grown or produced in this country, and most, or even all of it, has to be imported.

Did you know?

Children were urged to help save food. *The Win-the-War Cookery Book* declared: 'The child who saves bread is a soldier too.'

Germany tried to starve us out using her U-boats (submarines), sinking ships entering British waters; this caused problems when the ship in question was a neutral one. By January 1915 eggs were getting scarce, magazines had adverts for various egg substitutes. *Home Cookery In War-Time* advised: 'The many substitutes for eggs are useful when custards have to be provided cheaply in large quantities for healthy and hungry children.'

Above left: Wheat shortages led to bread shortages, and the nation was urged to cut back on bread to help defeat the U-boats. Posters such as this were everywhere; some advocated having an extra potato instead of bread.

Above right: The Food Controller was the title given to what we would call the Minister of Food, although in the home, Mother was certainly the food controller.

Germany restrained its U-boat activities for the first half of the war, but in 1917 Germany declared that any ships entering the area of their blockade would be liable to be sunk. Shipping losses soared to 300,000 tons per month in 1917. Food shortages became acute; mothers were urged, 'Get your children on your side in the food battle. The children can help win the war. Children, as well as grown-ups, waste food ... make it clear to them that they, too, are now in the fighting line, and they will help to fight.'

In January 1917 the Government created the Ministry of Food to oversee the nation's food supplies, led by the 'Food Controller', Lord Devonport. Under the Ministry, Local Food Committees were set up to oversee the supply of basic foods in their area. There was need to cut down on the amount we ate; official advice was to always leave the table hungry. A *Punch* cartoon had a young boy saying to his mother; 'I don't know how it is, but I never seem to get that nice sick feeling nowadays.' The Ministry of Food insisted that puddings made with milk were not necessary except for children, and should only be sparingly provided. While porridge, if not made too thick, was quite palatable without milk.

In response to food shortages the government allowed local authorities to turn unused land into allotments. For many a man the allotment became his war work, as is shown in this parody of a famous recruiting poster.

By February 1917, there was a nationwide shortage of potatoes, a product we do grow a lot of, but a blight decimated the harvest. From April the Ministry of Food announced that there were to be five potato-less days a week; all except Wednesdays and Fridays. Shops could not sell potatoes on these days, and the public were encouraged not to eat them. Rice was recommended as a substitute; popularly served as rice balls, or sieved to look like mashed potato.

The huge increase in land given over to allotments, and the popularity and ease of growing potatoes on them, ended the crisis: by July the shortage was over, and potato-less days were cancelled.

With wheat being one of our biggest imports, supplying our daily bread became a problem. *The Win-the-War Cookery Book* urged mothers to 'teach your children to eat slowly, you do them a service from which they will benefit all their lives long. Above all teach them to chew their bread till it is sweet in the mouth.'

WHEN FATHER SAYS DIG, WE ALL DIG.

Above: Working on the allotment, or in the vegetable garden, became an activity in which all the family could be involved, although, unlike the kitchen, here Dad was the boss.

Right: By 1917 it was becoming clear that voluntary rationing was not working, and local rationing was set up, although it would not be until the following year that national rationing was introduced.

WAR RATIONS

Keep on Smiling
        Dont look Glum
Half a Loaf
        Is better than None.

The shortage of bread was a particular problem for the poor, for whom it made up a large part of their diet. In January 1917 to maximise the use of flour, the Food Controller issued an order prohibiting the use of white flour. Wholemeal bread, made to strict standards, became the order of the day. The official name for the new bread was G.R Bread – the initials standing for 'Government regulation' – but it was commonly known as 'war bread'. The Ministry of Food told anxious parents that the flour 'contains more lime and is therefore better suited for growing children than fine wheaten flour'. By November another Government order was made allowing the use of potatoes in bread-making – up to one-eighth of the weight.

Early in 1918 the Government introduced 'meatless days' on which no meat, cooked or uncooked, could be sold. Suggested alternatives included 'Thick Vegetable Soup', 'Savoury Vegetable Stew', and 'Stuffed Parsnips and Potatoes'. There were also calls from some quarters for all non-working dogs to be put down to save meat.

Importing, as we did, all our sugar, it soon became a problem; people were encouraged to do without, and eating sweets was seen as unpatriotic. As an alternative to sweets, children might be offered the dubious treat of chocolate biscuits made from a mixture of flour, cocoa

Below left: To solve the problem of meat shortages the government introduced meatless days in April 1917. On the weekly designated day, no meat could be served in eating places, or sold in shops.
Below right: Meat shortages brought calls for the destruction of all dogs, except 'working dogs'. What constituted a working dog was a most contentious question.

All through a meatless day!

I'm not useless—I take care of our house !

butter, ground rice, sieved boiled potatoes, cocoa, egg and treacle. It became clear that voluntary action was not working, and, in late 1917, everyone had to register with a local shopkeeper and receive a sugar card, as a first step towards rationing.

Did you know?

In 1916 sweets became a rare treat; manufacturers were ordered to cut back production to half and then a quarter of the amount produced in 1915.

WAITER! WHERE IS MY PORTION OF SUGAR? IT WAS THERE JUST NOW SIR, I EXPECT THAT FLY MUST HAVE EATEN IT.

The amounts of shortage food items served in restaurants was a source of much humour, for example, 'Waiter', 'how did you find the steak?' Customer, 'I looked under a sprout and there it was.'

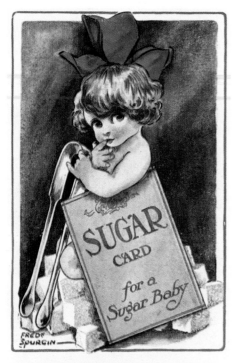

JUST ENOUGH TO COVER MY
BARE WANTS !

"Fancy eating sweets like that in War time!"
"Garn, fat 'ead! It's toofache!"

Above left: In 1917 sugar cards were issued as part of local rationing. They would provide, as the card says, 'just enough to cover my bare wants'.
Above right: Sugar was heavily controlled, and the sugar content of sweets and confectionery was curtailed. Eating sweets was seen as unpatriotic, as this card shows.

During 1917 the Ministry introduced the Food Economy Campaign; adults were asked to undergo voluntary rationing. Children were not included in the scheme, as the needs of the individual child differed widely. However, in December the Director of Food Economy issued a suggested rationing scale for children, of bread, cereals, meat, sugar and lard. Depending on their age, for instance, they would receive from 3 to 4½ lb of bread a week, and so on. Girls of 13 to 18 should receive no less than four-fifths of the ration for boys of the same age. Younger girls should receive the same quantities as boys. Children should be weighed every month at the same time of day before a meal, and a record kept. If their weight stayed the same or went down for two consecutive months, the allowance of food should be increased.

By December 1917, milk was short, and subsequently expensive. The Ministry, anticipating the shortage, had laid in a stock of full cream dried milk suitable for infant feeding. Medical Officers could obtain this milk for distribution to children at cost price, and many did so. Several local authorities took steps to ensure a supply of milk for young children by initiating schemes of milk distribution. Applications for milk had to be signed by the Medical Officer of Health, the medical officer of an infant welfare centre, or a general practitioner; priority tickets were then issued for children up to five

An ice cream vendor, just before the war. Like many other treats, the sight of the ice cream man's cart would become increasingly rare as the war went on.

years old, along with a card showing the weekly amounts of milk allotted. These were then handed to the officially designated dairyman, and the amount supplied marked on the card.

There were no ice cream vans; instead, ice cream sellers used bicycles with a large box at the front, usually with a wheel each side, or a hand cart. The box was insulated to keep the ice cream inside cold. 'Stop me and buy one' might well be written on the side, along with the maker's name. A lot of ice cream sellers were Italian immigrants, and produced what was variously known as 'hokey-cokey', or hokey-pokey' ice cream. Many children would ask for the 'penny lick'; the vendor would scoop some of the ice cream into a small glass bowl rather than a cornet, and the children would lick the ice cream from the bowl. When they had finished they would return the bowl to the ice cream man, which he would dip in a pail of water and then use it to serve the next customer! With milk and sugar shortages, they became a rare sight during the war.

In January 1918 the London food committees asked the food controller to introduce a rationing scheme for the whole of London and the Home Counties, which was published one month later. At the end of February a rationing scheme for meat, butter and margarine for London, Middlesex, Hertfordshire, Essex, Surrey, Sussex, and Kent was introduced.

Everybody received two cards – one for meat and one for butter and margarine; the latter having spaces for other items to be added if required. There were separate cards for adults and children. On the cards were a series of numbered coupons each representing one quarter of a week's ration. With the meat card these had to be torn off by the shopkeeper with whom you were registered when you exchanged them for your meat ration – you could only get your ration from the supplier you were registered with. On the butter and margarine card the

London and Home Counties. CHILD'S MEAT CARD. D 8.
(See Instructions overleaf).

Butcher's Name ____________

Butcher's Address ____________

GIVE THIS PART TO YOUR BUTCHER

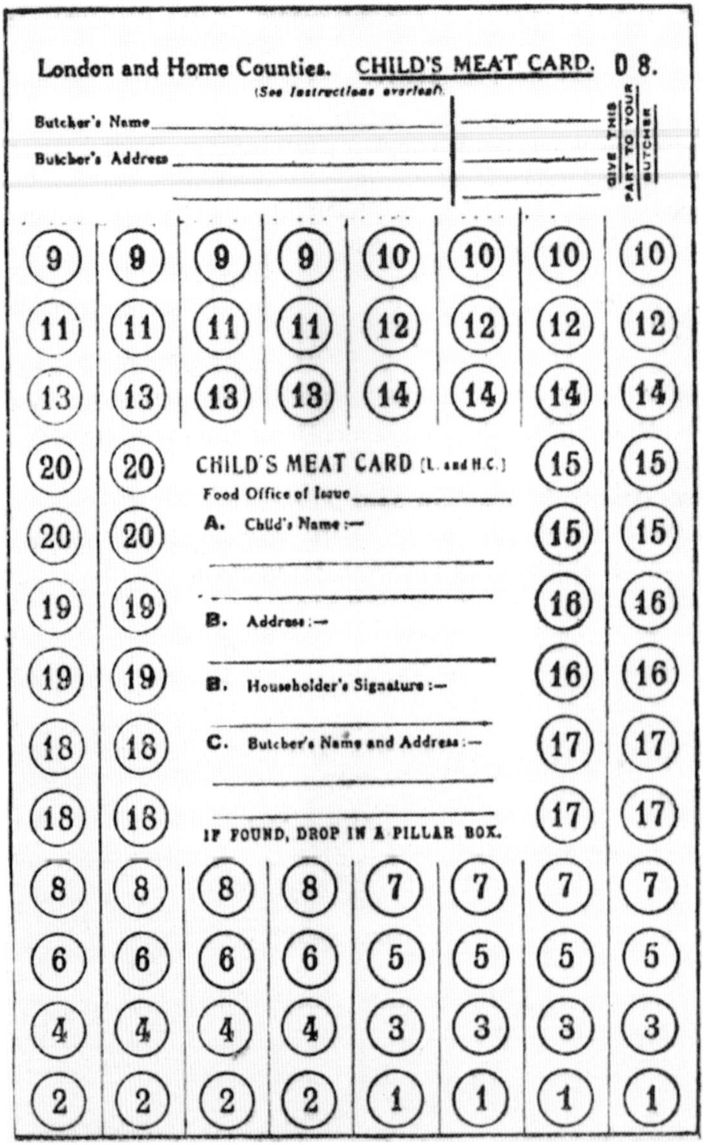

9	9	9	9	10	10	10	10
11	11	11	11	12	12	12	12
13	13	13	13	14	14	14	14
20	20					15	15
20	20					15	15
19	19					16	16
19	19					16	16
18	18					17	17
18	18					17	17
8	8	8	8	7	7	7	7
6	6	6	6	5	5	5	5
4	4	4	4	3	3	3	3
2	2	2	2	1	1	1	1

CHILD'S MEAT CARD (L. and H.C.)

Food Office of Issue ____________

A. Child's Name :—

B. Address :—

B. Householder's Signature :—

C. Butcher's Name and Address :—

IF FOUND, DROP IN A PILLAR BOX.

A local rationing meat card for a child in the London and Home Counties area. Variations on the card were issued in all areas in late 1917, early 1918.

coupons were crossed off by the retailer as they were used. Under this scheme, every adult was entitled to 1*s* 8*d*-worth of meat each week; children under six were allowed only half that. Both adults and children were limited to a quarter pound of either butter or margarine, later increased to 1 oz of butter and 4 oz of margarine.

In February 1918, the Ministry recommended creamed dripping as 'especially good for children'; 'Take 2 oz of clarified dripping, 1 dessert-spoonful of milk and ½ teaspoonful of honey. Cream the dripping thoroughly till quite soft and white with a wooden spoon. Add the milk drop by drop and beat it in, preferably with a whisk; lastly add the honey and beat it thoroughly. Set aside till it becomes firm.'

The London scheme was extended to the whole country from April. In mid-July the first national ration books were issued, to last for sixteen weeks, followed by a second ration book in October.

Once again, customers had to register with suppliers for sugar, fats, butcher's meat, and bacon; this could be several different suppliers or a single one for everything. Inside the ration book were pages of numbered and named coupons – 'meat', etc., plus 'spare' coupons; this meant that new items could be rationed at any time without the need of producing a new book. To avoid confusion, coupons for different items were in different colours; meat – red; butter & margarine – blue; sugar – yellow, etc. As with the earlier butter and margarine cards, coupons were cut (or torn) out as they were used, or a page or pages of coupons could be removed and deposited with the retailer.

There were special green ration books for children under six years old, containing two pages of meat coupons instead of the four pages in the general books. The child's meat coupons had the same value the adult's, but once again only half as many coupons were issued to a child. Babies received a green book as soon as possible after the birth to give the mother extra food while she was nursing.

The cover of a child's national ration book from October 1918, with its distinctive green cover. This was the second national rationing book, the first having been issued in April 1918.

MINISTRY OF FOOD.
CHILD'S RATION BOOK (A).

INSTRUCTIONS.

Read carefully these instructions and the leaflet which will be sent you with this Book.

1. The parent or guardian of the child named on the reference leaf as the holder of this ration book must sign his own name and write the child's name and address in the space below, and write the child's name and address, and the serial number (printed upside down on the back cover) in the space provided to the left of each page of coupons.

WEST HAM

Food Office of } Issue .... Date....Oct 18....

Signature of Child's } *Wm. Jones* Parent or Guardian }

Name of Child.... *Ivor R. Jones*

Address.... *24, Flora Rd, Forest Gate*

2. For convenience of writing at the Food Office the Reference Leaf has been put opposite the back cover, and has purposely been printed upside down. It should be carefully examined. If there is any mistake in the entries on the Reference Leaf, the Food Office should be asked to correct it.

3. The book must be registered at once by the child's parent or guardian, who must take the book to the retailers with whom the child was previously registered for butcher's meat, bacon, butter and margarine, sugar and tea respectively, or, if the child has not previously held a book, to any retailers chosen. These retailers must write their names and the addresses of their shops in the proper space on the back of the cover. The books of children staying in hotels, boarding houses, hostels, schools and similar establishments should not be registered until they leave the establishment.

4. The ration book may be used only by or on behalf of the holder, to buy rationed food for him, or members of the same household, or guests sharing common meals. It may not be used to buy rationed food for any other persons.

[*Continued on next page.*]

N. 1. (Nov.)

F. FOOD OFFICE. IF FOUND, RETURN TO ANY FOOD OFFICE.

HINTS ON ECONOMY—
Cultivate your own Cabbages.

Children would play a large part in growing your own food; at school many would grow food towards the school dinners on dug-over playgrounds and at home many, like this boy, would have a little corner of the garden.

There were also supplementary ration books. These would be given out, in addition to the ordinary book, to those who were regarded as needing extra food, such as heavy manual workers and boys (not girls) between the ages of thirteen and eighteen, whose supplementary books were coloured pink. Lads of eighteen who were preparing for military service continued to receive the supplementary rations until called up.

Children at boarding school had to take their ration books with them, and were registered with the school's suppliers. When returning home for Christmas or other holidays, the children had to use emergency cards with their home suppliers.

Under the general rationing scheme the amounts to which each child was entitled each week were roughly as follows: ½ lb of uncooked meat, 6 ozs of butter and margarine, 2 ozs of lard, 4 to 8 ozs of bacon and ham according to the district, and 8 ozs of sugar, 1½ ozs of cheese, and 1½ ozs of tea.

8
High Days and Holidays

As with most other areas of Edwardian life, there was a great deal of difference in the holiday experience of rich and poor children. Pre-war, well-to-do families might well go abroad for their holidays, but foreign travel was beyond the reach of most of the middle classes. The war virtually put a stop to foreign holidays; Europe was at war, and other places, such as America meant long sea journeys, and the threat of U-boats.

Most people went instead to British seaside resorts, some for just a day or two, many for a week. The Georgians had virtually invented the seaside holiday, but only for the wealthy. Now, the *charabanc* – the Edwardian equivalent of a minibus – and the railways meant that travel was within the reach of many more people; special cheap day train excursions were laid on during the holidays, and cheap boarding houses sprang up around popular holiday destinations that catered for the working classes on restricted budgets, such as Blackpool, Skegness, Margate, and Southend. There were also more 'genteel' holiday destinations where well-brought up children would not have to rub shoulders with street urchins.

In many working class areas, the summer holiday was a working one, where mother, granny and the children would spend a week or more working on a farm, picking the harvest; often joined at the weekend by dad, who had his regular job to do during the week. In London, for instance, many families would travel to Kent to pick hops in September. This was in school time; teachers would mark the pupil as 'hopping' in the register, giving us our modern expression 'hopping off school'. Whilst the amount of beer brewed was curtailed during the war, and subsequently, the amount of hops required, there was still a lot needed, making many jobs for women and children. In other places it might be apple or other fruit picking, or lifting potatoes or other vegetables. Often they would stay in huts or barns on the farm. While it was hard work, the fresh air of the countryside was a welcome break from the grimy city streets, and for most children, these family holidays were eagerly looked forward to. For the poorest children the only holiday might be spent in the local park, paddling in the pond.

The Seaside

Early in the war railway travel became restricted by the need to ship vast amounts of men and materials to France, but this soon died down and railway travel continued, although cheap fares and excursion rates were cancelled; the traveller suffered to some extent, although not so much as might have been expected.

Resorts on the south and east coasts became the targets of sea raids, such as that on Scarborough, Whitby, and Hartlepool in December 1914, and of Zeppelin raids, such as that on Great Yarmouth in January 1915, and many people went further north, or to the west coast.

Holiday-makers could enjoy a walk along the promenade, taking in the gardens which often to be found there, stopping at one of the many tea rooms or public houses and perhaps taking a trip on a pleasure boat. Another treat was to hear a band playing on the bandstand, or see a concert on the pier. On the beach, children would enjoy paddling and

Clacton-on-Sea

Above: Clacton-on-Sea. The turn of the century saw a boom in seaside holidays; here you can see several children, some with spades, some crab fishing, all quite formally dressed.

Left: The photograph is captioned 'Paignton August 1911'. The two young girls are wearing typical long-legged bathing costumes, similar to those worn by adults.

BY GUM! IT'S CHAMPION
AT BLACKPOOL,
NONE OF THOSE ZEPPELINS OR SUBMARINES HERE

IF I HAD ANOTHER
SIXPENCE I'D STAY
ANOTHER WEEK

A trip to the seaside in 1916 might well be seen as a holiday from the war, especially from Zeppelin raids, although, despite the lady's comment, you might well be close to a submarine.

swimming, making sandcastles, having donkey-rides and watching a Punch and Judy show. Shrimping was popular, using a net on a pole to trawl pools, sometimes catching small crabs and other creatures.

By now early slot machines were appearing in arcades, such as the mutoscope showing short films, often of the 'what the butler saw' type. There were also funfair rides, such as helter-skelters, carousels and big wheels. Another attraction, popular with the children, was a miniature railway; a small-scale train, though still big enough to ride on, which might go along the sea-front.

Empire Day

This was a day designed to 'remind children that they formed part of the British Empire, and that they might think with others in lands across the sea, what it meant to be sons and daughters of such a glorious Empire'. The first Empire Day took place on 24 May 1902, the year following Queen Victoria's death, on the anniversary of her birthday. Many schools across the British Empire celebrated it, although it was not officially recognised until 1916. That year, Empire Day was celebrated throughout the country, and in most instances school children were given a half-holiday in order to take part in marches, concerts, maypole dances, and parties. They would salute the flag, sing 'God Save the King' and other patriotic songs, and chant 'Remember Empire Day, the 24th of May'. In the evenings there were often huge bonfires and fireworks, just like Guy Fawkes Night, although the war would have a deep effect on this element of both events.

Guy Fawkes

The Defence of the Realm Act banned bonfires or fireworks at night as part of the lighting restrictions. However on 5 November 1914 some relaxation of the rules was allowed for small fireworks in certain areas. In 1915 the rules were further relaxed, permitting limited firework displays if permission was obtained from the authorities. As the raiding got worse, so bonfires disappeared, and with them went one of the children's favourites; potatoes baked in the embers of the bonfire, split open and a hunk of butter put inside. Burnt and sooty on the outside, they somehow managed to taste delicious. A cheap alternative to fireworks were the raids themselves; children, as well as adults, watched the spectacle of searchlights sweeping the sky, and if they found a Zepp, the flashes of the anti-aircraft shells exploding around it.

Some youngsters who worked in munitions factories managed to smuggle out detonators, which exploded with a loud report when hit with a brick or a rock, however the local police and magistrates took a dim view of this if the culprits were caught.

Empire Day certificate 1916. Empire Day, celebrating the British Empire, had been celebrated unofficially for some years, but in 1916 it became official. These certificates were awarded to boys and girls who had sent gifts to servicemen.

Carrying out the Police Regulations:
Fitting Dark Blinds to her Sitting Room.

Above left: Lighting restrictions, later to be known as the blackout, would severely limit the use of bonfires and firework displays in the towns and cities.

Above right: Guy Fawkes Night; a pre-war guy. As the war went on there was some relaxation of the lighting restrictions for bonfires, but fireworks were hard to get.

Christmas

The first Christmas of the war was, on the whole, a sober one. After the scare of the early German advances the war situation was no longer immediately menacing, but the widespread belief that it would be 'all over by Christmas' was obviously wrong, and the future far from clear. For many children that year, the greatest present would be their father home on leave for Christmas; in the event, few servicemen enjoyed a Christmas leave that year, leaving hundreds of thousands of empty seats around the dinner table.

By Christmas 1915, however, with the growing army of Britain in France and Flanders, there were thousands of fighters whose leave was due; so many so that lots were drawn by the troops, the winners getting a week or ten day's leave in 'Blighty'. Not only would that mean Dad home for Christmas, but the possibility of a grand Christmas present in the form of a souvenir from the front; perhaps even the most desired one – a German helmet!

By 1916 war-weariness had set in, and a grim attitude was pervasive. What with air raids, casualty lists, and shortages of food and other things, many felt that there was little to celebrate. *The War Illustrated* gave its response to this:

It's the kiddies' affair, and whether it gives you the pip or not, you've got to jolly well do your bit, and see that the kids have it! My children will keep the season as a Church

Above left: For many families the best Christmas present would come in the form of a week's Christmas leave for Dad, or some other member of the family.
Above right: Cards from exotic places from members of the family or friends serving abroad were a feature of wartime Christmases. This one from Macedonia, 1917

festival, and I shall try to make it as bright as possible for them, but as far as extra food is concerned they most certainly will get nothing more than a slightly richer pudding than on usual days with "a fire round it", but I am afraid that there will be no crackers and, no snapdragon. The bread and the cakes will be made of war flour, and baking-powder and egg substitutes will take the place of eggs in the cakes; almonds and raisins and chocolates and sugar icing will be things of memory only, though I do think that we may manage a few chestnuts and oranges.

Did you know?

Mothers and children worked together selecting gifts and treats, making comforts, and packing Christmas parcels for their fathers and other loved ones in the trenches.

By Christmas 1917, many of the traditional ingredients for Christmas dinner were scarce – turkeys and chickens, for instance; so much so that in many of the poorer districts of London, instead of selling whole birds, dealers sold turkeys and chickens in quarter 'cuts'. The use of dried fruits in the cake and the pudding had to be cut back, as did the flour; owing to the reduced tonnage of shipping, the country had smaller stocks of currants and raisins than we needed. The Ministry of Food came out with recipes for 'Wartime Christmas pudding', made with a large proportion of potato, and 'Mincemeat for patriotic people', yet few children were fooled by the patriotic names; they just didn't taste anywhere near as good as 'the real thing'.

Presents, too, were severely limited, so many toy factories having gone over to making munitions. It had been usual for poorer children to be given home-made gifts; now this became the norm for many of their better-off cousins.

Christmas Parties

For the first Christmas of the war, 1914, it was common for local groups or councils to pay for a party for all the school children whose fathers and brothers were away serving their country. One typical party held in Crieff, in Scotland, for instance, entertained over two hundred such children; they had a 'sumptuous' tea, followed by a conjurer – one of whose tricks was, topically, to change of a number of small Allied flags into one huge Union Jack stretching the entire length of the platform. This was followed by the presentation of gifts, in addition to which, the children each received an apple, an orange, and a Christmas cracker.

By Christmas 1917 food shortages meant sumptuous meals were out of the question. The Food Controller (later called the Minister of Food) set out guidance for Children's Parties:

Such entertainments fall naturally into two classes – those in which amusement is the main consideration and refreshments are merely incidental, and those in which a good meal for the poor is the main object. In the first case refreshments should as far as possible be entirely dispensed with; in the second the food provided should consist as far as possible of non-essential foodstuffs, and care should be taken to avoid those articles of which there is a temporary shortage, such as tea. Whilst Lord Rhondda has no wish entirely to curtail entertainments, especially those given at Christmastime for

A patriotic Christmas gift might come in the form of a National Savings card, complete with a few stamps inside. By 1917 special cards like this were being produced.

> ### THE NATION'S WAR TIME CHRISTMAS CARD.
> ———
> Lord God of Hosts, be with us yet.
> Lest we forget—lest we forget!
>
> Kipling.
> ———
>
> ## With Hearty Greetings for Christmas and the New Year.
>
> From ....

the benefit of children or of soldiers and sailors, he desires they should only be given provided the catering is on the lines suggested above, and that in every case the utmost care is taken to prevent waste and to economise in all foodstuffs.

End of the War
The shortages of food and other commodities from which Britain suffered were, in fact, fairly mild compared with Germany. The Royal Navy's blockade was far more effective than that of the U-boats, and by late 1918 her civilian population were on the verge of starvation and revolt; Germany had to sue for peace.

The peace which broke out on 11 November 1918 was not actually a peace but a ceasefire, or Armistice. This did not stop celebrations from taking place; over four years of bloody war had come to an end, and the relief and joy could not be held back. Most schools announced a holiday, or at least a half-holiday to commemorate the end of fighting.

The peace conference, comprising delegates from thirty-two countries, first met in Paris in January 1919 to hammer out a peace treaty. In spite of the large amount of nations involved, the conference was actually dominated by the 'Big Four'; Prime Minister David Lloyd George, France's Prime Minister Georges 'Tiger' Clemenceau, Vittorio Orlando of Italy and US President Woodrow Wilson.

I WAS NEARLY SQUEEZED TO DEATH IN THE CROWD!

They wanted very different things; Clemenceau, on whose country much of the war had been fought, wanted to punish Germany severely; Wilson wanted a new world of international understanding through a new group, the League of Nations, with Lloyd George somewhere in between. He managed to persuade Clemenceau to agree to the League of Nations and a more lenient peace treaty than the Tiger wanted, and to persuade Wilson to agree to the War Guilt Clause under which Germany would accept responsibility for starting the war.

In March the German representatives were shown the proposed treaty, which they had to sign or go back to war; there was no negotiation. On 28 June 1919, the conference met at the Hall of Mirrors in Versailles, near Paris, where the two German delegates had

The news of the Armistice was greeted by wild celebrations. Parades and street parties took place up and down the country in November 1918.

no option but to sign. The War was over at last; by this point many of the youngest children could not remember a time of peace.

In Britain the official Peace Day celebrations were held on Saturday 19 July 1919. Celebrations were organised all over the country, with parades, concerts and street parties, and in the evening, bonfires and firework displays. Often, the local celebrations went on much longer; in Southampton, for instance, there were events over the following week, including, on the Saturday itself, a royal salute fired by the Hampshire Royal Artillery, followed by a parade supported by the regimental band, two sports meetings; one for boys attending secondary and private schools, and a separate one for girls. In the evening a parade including the local scouts, sea scouts, the boys' life brigade, boys from the seamans' orphanage, girl guides, the girls' brigade, local school cadets, and members of the Sunday schools union.

PARISH OF HORNCHURCH

.. THE ..

PEACE ✱ CELEBRATIONS

WILL BE HELD ON

SATURDAY, AUGUST 9th, 1919

In the FIELD BETWEEN HARROW DRIVE and GREY TOWERS CAMP

(By kind permission of the Officer Commanding)

OLD FOLKS AND WIDOWS DINNER

(Provided by W. Varco Williams, Esq., J.P., C.C.), at 1 p.m. in the DRILL HALL, High Street, Hornchurch.

NOTE. *Persons over 60 years of age and all widows desirous of attending must send in their names at once to the Clerk to the Council, Billet Lane, Hornchurch, when an invitation will be sent them.*

FANCY DRESS CARNIVAL

(Arranged by the D. & D. S. & S. Federation) Commencing at 2 p.m. Parade outside the Parish Church. Eight Classes, 16 Prizes.

Class 1 INDIVIDUAL ENTRIES LADIES		Class 6 DECORATED PERAMBULATORS.
Class 2 do. GENTLEMEN.		Class 7 DECORATED HORSES AND CARTS, CARS,
Class 3 LADIES TABLEAUX.		LORRIES, etc.
Class 4 GENTLEMEN'S TABLEAUX.		Class 8 DECORATED CYCLES AND MOTOR CYCLES,
Class 5 SCHOOL CHILDREN.		etc.

Entries for the above to be sent to Mr. C. BULLOCK, 2 The Avenue, Hornchurch, by August 6th

GAMES AND RACES

COMMENCING AT 2.30 P.M.

1 Parade of Carnival	7 Egg and Spoon Race, under 14, Handicap	14 Tug-of-War, teams of 9
2 100yds. Flat Race, over 14 years of age, Scratch	8 Bun Struggle	15 Ladies' and Gentlemen's Blindfold Driving Race
3 100yds. Flat Race, under 14 years of age, Handicap	9 Obstacle Race, Open	16 Four-legged Race
4 Long Distance Race of about 3 miles	10 100yds. Veteran Race, over 60 years of age, Handicap	17 Sweep and Miller Fight
5 Sack Race, 50yds. open	11 Derby Race, Jockeys under 6 years	18 Wrestling on Horseback, Teams of six pairs
6 Egg and Spoon Race, over 14	12 Tilting the Bucket	
	13 Obstacle Race, open to Members of D.D.S.S. Federation	

Good Prizes. Entries free, open to residents of Hornchurch only (including Camp), should be posted to Mr. H. Sell, Hon. Sec. to Fete Committee, 94 Craigdale Road, Romford, by Wednesday, Aug. 6th. Children's Entries on Ground.

DANCING in DRILL HALL from 7.30 p.m. Admission 1/-

CONCERT in Marquee on Grounds, by the RONEO CONCERT PARTY at 7.30 p.m. Admission Free.

COUNTRY FAIR, SWINGS, ROUNDABOUTS, GUESSING COMPETITIONS, &c.

The Cottage Homes and Hornchurch Village Bands

WILL PLAY THROUGHOUT THE DAY

ADMISSION TO THE GROUNDS FREE. ➤ REFRESHMENTS AT POPULAR PRICES.

The signing of the Versailles treaty in July marked a second round of celebrations, like this one from Hornchurch in Essex, typical of many.

CHILDREN'S CELEBRATION

T. GARDNER, Esq., J.P., C.C. and Mrs. GARDNER having generously entertained the School Children of the South and Village Wards, and the North-West Committee the Children of the North-West Ward on the 24th July, no special provision for their entertainment will be made on this date.

(Signed) THE PEACE CELEBRATION COMMITTEE.

COUNCIL OFFICES, HORNCHURCH,
24th JULY, 1919.

Funds for the expenses of the Fete are urgently required, and contributions should be sent to Mr. C. H. Baker, Hon. Treas., High Street, Hornchurch, or W. C. Allen, Clerk to the Council, Billet Lane, Hornchurch.

GIFTS FOR PRIZES WILL ALSO BE WELCOMED. Wilson and Whitworth Ltd., Printers, Romford.

On the 21st, children in the local infants' schools were presented with commemoration medals before marching to various centres for a celebration tea, followed by daylight fireworks, balloons and maroons, Punch and Judy shows, and music. Later the whole town was treated to a grand pageant entitled 'Britannia and her sons – a peace pageant of English history', in which many local schools and other groups took part, each presenting tableaux showing famous scenes and characters from British history. On the 22nd, a similar event took place for the local senior school children; this time there were also sports events.

For many children, the real end to the war only came when 'Daddy' at last came home, but for many hundreds of thousands of British children Daddy would never come home at all.

Did you know?

The End of the war was not the end of rationing. Meat rationing continued until 1919; butter until May 1920, and sugar until November 1920.

WE'LL ALL BE GLAD, DEAR SOLDIER LAD
WHEN YOU RETURN HOME SAFE ONCE MORE
AND HERE'S A VIEW TO SHOW TO YOU
THE WELCOME YOU'LL GET AT THE OLD FRONT DOOR!

Peace meant not only the end of hostilities, but also the return of loved ones. Many thought this would happen immediately, but with millions in the forces, the Government ran a phased demobilisation.

9
What Now?

If you've enjoyed the book you may wish to learn more about the subject.

Museums

Most local museums include sections on children, and the First World War; here are a few specialist museums you may wish to visit:

Imperial War Museum London, Lambeth Road, SE1 6HZ and Imperial War Museum North, Trafford Wharf Road, Manchester M17 1TZ; both have extensive First World War collections and feature regular special exhibitions. You can also search their collections online using www.iwm.org.uk/.

The V&A Museum of Childhood, Cambridge Heath Road, London E2 9PA, an annex of the V&A in Bethnal Green, contains childhood artefacts going back hundreds of years; it also features special exhibitions.

Similarly, Sudbury Hall & Museum of Childhood (National Trust), Main Road, Ashbourne, DE6 5HT, holds a large collection of artefacts. It also features a Victorian classroom, as does the Ragged School Museum, 46–50 Copperfield Road, London E3 4RR, which looks at life for the poorest children in Victorian times.

Smaller toy museums include the London Toy and Model Museum, 21–23 Craven Hill, London, W2 3EN, the Brighton Toy and Model Museum, 52–55 Trafalgar St, Brighton, and Pollock's Toy Museum, 1 Scala St, Fitzrovia, London W1T 2HL.

Further Reading

For further reading there are a plethora of modern books on the First World War, but beware, most cover the military side. Websites of interest include http://www.educationengland.org.uk/history/, which covers the history of education in depth.

Napoo—tootle-oo---
goodbye-ee!

There are several children's books from the period well worth reading, including; *The Secret Garden* by Frances Hodgson Burnett (pub. 1910), *The Railway Children*, by E. Nesbit (pub. 1906), plus many modern books, such as *Warhorse* by Michael Morpurgo (pub. 1982).

Collecting

Many of the illustrations that we've used in this book are either period postcards or artefacts. Such postcards, comic or photographic, can often be purchased for under £10 – often under £5 – from postcard shops and dealers. There are specialist postcard shops, and several regular postcard fairs organised up and down the country; organised by groups such as the Postcard Traders Association. These can be easily found on the internet under 'Postcard Fairs'. Condition is everything, so try to avoid buying cards with creases, tears, or surface damage. Look also at the back; a franked stamp will help to date it, and the message written on the back can be the prize – one card showing a Zeppelin coming down in flames read; 'We watched this, it looked just like this.'

Artefacts such as ration books, cards, etc., can also often be bought for less than £10 from ephemera fairs and militaria fairs, as well as on online auction sites. Once again, condition is the key to building a good collection; in the long run it is better to buy one excellent thing than three in poor condition. Old comics, books and magazines such as those mentioned in the book can also be picked up fairly cheaply, and the articles and adverts inside can be fascinating, and often (unintentionally) hilarious. Be careful with comics though; several were reproduced in the 1970s but there are no obvious marks to indicate this – don't pay much unless you are sure.

Happy hunting!